IMAGES
of England

NEWARK
AND DISTRICT

Newark, Kirkgate.

A view along Kirkgate that looks away from the parish church, around 1920. The Edwardian post office can be seen to the left, almost facing a group of timber-framed houses dating from four centuries earlier.

IMAGES
of England

NEWARK
AND DISTRICT

Compiled by
David Ottewell

TEMPUS

First published 1999
Copyright © David Ottewell, 1999

Tempus Publishing Limited
The Mill, Brimscombe Port,
Stroud, Gloucestershire, GL5 2QG

ISBN 0 7524 1816 5

Typesetting and origination by
Tempus Publishing Limited
Printed in Great Britain by
Midway Clark Printing, Wiltshire

The Newark coat of arms.

Contents

An Edwardian view of Lombard Street.

Acknowledgements

Thanks are due to the members of staff at Nottinghamshire Local Studies Library for their knowledgeable advice and help.

Although every attempt has been made to contact the relevant copyright holders, the age of some of the photographs used has in many cases made this impossible. If I have inadvertently missed anyone out I apologize. I will undertake to make amendments in future editions.

Introduction

The town of Newark owes its importance to its geographical position. Situated on the River Trent, it attracts both the people who use the river and more importantly those who wish to cross it. As a major navigable waterway the Trent has always been used for commercial purposes, transporting goods quickly and effectively. Over the last century or so, with the increase in leisure time, it has also proved a magnet for those wishing to spend time either on, in or by water. Newark caters for these river users.

Similarly, Newark is situated close to a major road intersection with the Fosse Way (A46), which runs west to east, crossing over the Great North Road (A1), which runs north to south. The importance of Newark is also reflected by the presence of two railway stations in the town, even today.

The history of Newark has been long and varied. Its name is thought to derive from the Danish 'Neu Wark' which translates as 'new fortress'. Being situated close to the Roman Fosse Way, it is not surprising that there is evidence of Roman settlement in the town. Newark was a much more important place in Saxon times. Archaeologists have unearthed a number of relics from this period and the general layout of the town can be traced back to this time. From the Norman period there is more written evidence of Newark's development, though there is still controversy over when the first castle might have been constructed by the river in the town. It is agreed that Bishop Alexander of Lincoln did order the building of a significant castle in Newark around 1129. Designed more as impressive living quarters than a strong defensive fortress, it nevertheless cemented Newark's importance.

During the English Civil War in the 1640s Newark sided with King Charles I. His ultimate defeat led to much of the castle being demolished. However, many buildings from this period still remain in the town.

Much of Newark's wealth was based on the fertile surrounding countryside. The products of the farms were transported, via the good local road network, to Newark where they were sold and ultimately processed. There were successful local milling, tanning and malting industries, and many local companies also specialized in supplying and repairing equipment for the agricultural market. The money that these trades brought into Newark is reflected in the range of eighteenth- and nineteenth-century buildings in the town. Many of these fine buildings thankfully survive to this day.

Newark has been well served by a number of capable and enterprising photographers who have recorded the development of the town and the lives of its citizens over the years. Amongst these were Henry Davage, Samuel Whiles and Frank Robinson. On a smaller scale M.E. Summers, J. and M. Simpson and a Mr Richards made contributions. From a little further afield H. Barrett of Southwell and A.W. Bourne of Leicester took some interesting photographs. In addition, national companies such as Francis Frith of Reigate, J. Valentine of Dundee and Raphael Tuck of London produced large runs of postcards featuring Newark.

It is from the sources mentioned above that many of the images used in this book have been chosen. Without their hard work, skill and foresight we would not have such a complete picture of Newark over the last 100 years.

Beaumond Cross, Newark. No. 2421.

Beaumond Cross, *c. 1925*. The Beaumond Cross was thought to have been built in the fourteenth century and stood proudly at the junction of Cartergate, Albert Street and Lombard Street until 1974.

One
North-West Newark

The bridge over the River Trent, looking into Newark. The first bridge over the river was a wooden structure built sometime after 1135 on the instructions of Bishop Alexander. Other wooden bridges followed until 1775 when the Duke of Newcastle had a stone bridge built.

The bridge over the River Trent, looking away from Newark. The 1775 stone bridge soon proved inadequate but instead of knocking it down the parapets were demolished and the bridge was widened. This took place in 1848-49 after which the bridge was able to cope with increased usage.

For many years the town's cattle market was held in the grounds of the castle. However, towards the end of the nineteenth century, it was decided to provide a purpose-built site. The new cattle market was opened on 20 April 1886.

The first station to be opened in Newark was the Midland station on the Nottingham to Lincoln line, which came into service on 3 August 1846. This photograph was taken in Edwardian times.

The Midland station is known as Newark Castle station because of its location. It catered for its last steam train in 1968.

Built in a mock-Tudor style to the design of architects Ernest, George and Peto, the Ossington Coffee Palace was an impressive building with varied accommodation that included stabling for over forty horses.

Viscountess Ossington of Ossington Hall had the Coffee Palace built in 1882 as a memorial to her late husband who had held the position of speaker of the House of Commons until 1872.

Looking up Beastmarket Hill, *c.* 1904. The building immediately under the church spire is the eighteenth-century Warwick House. At one time it was the home of Samuel Sketchley who many consider the father of the Newark brewing industry.

NWK 80   View from the Bridge, Newark

Eventually Warwick House was sold and became a garage known as Castle Motors which specialized in the sale of Vauxhall cars and Bedford trucks. In 1972 another change of usage occurred when Holden's took it over and converted it into the furniture shop of today.

Beastmarket Hill at the junction of Castle Gate, *c.* 1904. A tranquil scene showing the position of the Gilstrap Library backing on to the castle.

The Gilstrap Free Library was designed by William Henman of Birmingham and built on a site fronting Castle Gate.

Looking along a traffic-free Castle Gate with the Gilstrap Free Library to the right, facing the Royal Oak and the Ram Hotel.

This postcard, published by Friths of Reigate, was used to send Seasons Greetings in December 1904 and shows the Royal Oak selling locally brewed Holes Ales. The Royal Oak was in competition with its larger neighbour the Ram Hotel.

Built in the 1770s the Ram Hotel was one of the premier coaching inns of Newark for many years. Coaches passed into the pub yard through the arch. By the 1930s this had been converted into a pedestrian entrance.

In an area of farmers, millers and maltsters, the Corn Exchange was an important building. It was built in the Italian baroque style at a cost of £6,000. Opening on 27 September 1848, it served the town until 1978.

Northgate House was built in the Georgian period. From the early nineteenth century it became the home of George Hodgkinson who was Mayor of Newark in 1826. It remained in the same family until 1912 when it was left for the use of the people of Newark. This is a rear view taken from the gardens.

Leaving Newark via Northgate you eventually reach the approach to the Great Northern railway station which was constructed in 1852.

The Great Northern station is Newark's main station, serving the line that runs from London to the North. It was opened in 1852 and has three platforms to cater for the daily influx of passengers.

This heavy horse and operative are thought to be standing in Newark Northgate station yard. For many years the original horsepower was used extensively around the station.

Two

Newark Castle

The main entrance to the castle was through the 800-year-old gatehouse which rises to 3 storeys high on the northern side of the courtyard.

This aerial view of the castle clearly shows its position on the eastern side of the river with the bridge giving east to west access.

THE CASTLE, NEWARK.

The castle observed from the opposite side of the Trent Navigation. Through the gates to the right were the New Gardens, which were disastrously flooded only a month after their official opening, much to the embarrassment of the Town Council.

Newark's favourable geographical situation encouraged Bishop Alexander of Lincoln to set out in 1129 on an extensive building programme in Newark. Small parts of this castle remain today, notably the gatehouse and the south-west tower.

Newark Castle during the Civil War. The town was loyal to the Royalist cause during the Civil War. It withstood three sieges before the Governor of the Castle, Lord Bessasis, followed Charles I's instructions and surrendered to the parliamentary forces on 8 May 1846.

Less than twenty per cent of the medieval castle remains today as much of it was destroyed on the orders of Parliament after the sieges in the Civil War.

THE CASTLE, NEWARK ON TRENT

The long west wall of Newark Castle still presents an imposing sight with the Trent running before it.

River & Castle, Newark on-Trent.

The 1990s have seen another concentrated period of excavation at Newark Castle which has revealed much new evidence about the development of the castle over the centuries.

The white wooden bridge, central to this picture, dates from 1827 when it was constructed to take the Trent Navigation towpath over the millrace.

The castle and the rear of Castle Gate from the Tolney Lane area. The Quibell Brothers' warehouse can be seen next to the castle and a little further along is the rear of the Corn Exchange.

An aerial view of Newark taken in the 1950s. The castle and the Trent are prominent in the foreground while St Mary's dominates the background.

The twelfth-century gatehouse of Newark Castle, seen from inside the castle grounds. The staircase turret to the right contains a circular staircase giving access to the upper floors.

Looking into the castle grounds, which were acquired by Newark Corporation in 1890. The corporation paid the Crown the sum of £500, which seems cheap by today's prices!

Once the corporation had purchased the castle grounds they proceeded to set them out as pleasure gardens with areas of grass, flowerbeds and paths.

A group of Edwardian citizens relax in the sun on the promenade within the castle grounds.

A postcard sent from the town in 1903 showing a view under the castle terrace. This was an area used for the more mundane aspects of castle life either as servant accommodation or storage space.

King John's Death Chamber, Newark Castle

The so-called King John's Death Chamber is in the south-west tower of the castle but, despite the name, it is unlikely that King John died in this room.

This corner of the castle was often used as a backdrop for group photographs. Those featured here are No. 1 Section of 8th Depot Co., Royal Engineers, who visited the castle while training in the area during the First World War.

Mr John Mountney, seen here in the cap feeding the pigeons, looked after a small museum in the castle grounds. He was often found entertaining visitors to the castle.

GREAT NORTH ROAD SHOWING CASTLE, NEWARK-ON-TRENT

A fine collection of 1940s cars parked on the northern side of the castle. The road continues into the distance as it crosses the bridge over the Trent.

J.W. Ruddock of Lincoln published a set of four postcards of paintings by Fanny Easterfield including this one of the castle grounds. Peacocks were introduced to the castle when the pleasure grounds were developed in 1889.

The Castle Gardens, Newark

On Saturday 3 July 1912 the Duchess of Newcastle opened a new area of public gardens which the Town Council had set out in meadowland on the banks of the Trent facing Newark Castle. The focal point of the park was an eighteenth-century sundial (seen behind the chair) which had once belonged to William Dickinson, a noted local historian.

The site of the new park proved a bad choice as only a month after the opening a freak storm resulted in the Trent bursting its banks and flooding the park. Wits among the locals renamed the gardens 'Luny Park'. Notice the position of the sundial in the flood water.

Three
The River Trent

CASTLE & TRENT BRIDGE, NEWARK ON TRENT.

The Trent with Trent Bridge in the foreground and beyond it the frontage of the castle standing on the eastern bank of the river.

The artist Fanny H. Easterfield has managed to include Trent Bridge, Ossington Coffee House and St Mary's church in this picture.

Situated adjacent to the castle and fronting the Trent Navigation was the warehouse belonging to the well-known Newark firm, Quibell Brothers.

The Trent Navigation has been a very busy waterway for many years. The Edwardian era was no exception as can be seen from this view taken a little down from the castle.

Like other parts of the national canal system, as the Trent Navigation became less used for transporting goods, it took on a new role as a waterway for pleasure craft. Such boats can be seen here passing through Newark Lock.

Newark's close proximity to the River Trent has resulted in the town being flooded on a number of occasions. These floods occurred in December 1910.

Close to the Victorian hall at Kelham, the narrow Kelham Hall Bridge provides a route across the river for traffic, even today.

Henry Davage of Kirkgate produced this postcard of Jobson's boathouse, which was situated at the mouth of the River Devon.

River Devon and Rowing Club, Newark-on-Trent.

A variety of pleasure craft are tied up on either bank of the river in this 1950s postcard of the River Devon and Rowing Club.

A deserted scene showing the River Trent above Newark Lock. The river would often be busy with pleasure craft or larger boats carrying cargoes.

An advertising postcard for Herbert Jobson's business where, in addition to building and repairing boats, he hired out motor boats and rowing boats and took people for trips on the river.

The Old Water Mill. Before the days of electricity water and wind were both important sources of power.

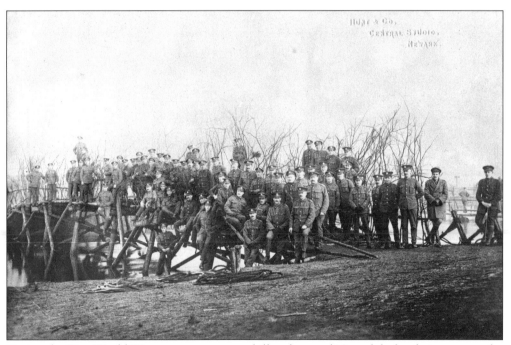

During the First World War many troops were billeted around Newark before being sent to the front in France. Often one of their training exercises was to erect a temporary bridge such as this one which was put up in the course of one night in February 1918.

The bridge over the River Devon is an ancient crossing point dating back to at least the eleventh century. For many years it was known as Markham Bridge. To cross the river a fee was paid to the toll-keeper who lived in a cottage on the Farndon side of the bridge.

The weir at Newark is crossed by the Longstone Bridge. In the background is the Trent Brewery, one of the oldest of the town's maltings, which was run by Richardson, Earp and Slater in the latter part of the nineteenth century. These buildings were demolished in 1952.

Four
Religion

As this 1940s view of Kirkgate illustrates, the parish church of St Mary Magdalene occupies a most prominent position in Newark. Its tower and spire stand 240ft 8in tall and can be seen from far and wide. It is considered to be one of the largest parish churches in the country.

The parish church of St Mary Magdalene. There has been a church on this site since at least Saxon times. The present building was begun in the twelfth century with a variety of developments and additions taking place over the years. A major restoration took place in 1853.

The War Memorial to commemorate the local dead in two World Wars was unveiled in the grounds of the parish church.

The plans for London Road Congregational church were drawn up by Nottingham architect, Henry Harper. The original Congregational church on London Road was a temporary structure known as the 'Tin Tabernacle' which was opened on 1 September 1889.

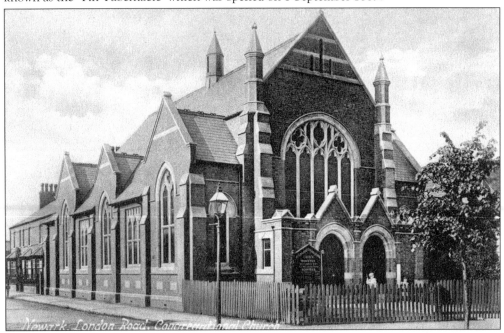

London Road Congregational church was constructed between 1907 and 1908 and formally opened on 12 March 1908. It is interesting to compare the actual building with the plan above.

St Leonard's church was situated on Northgate. It was built using local stone and opened on 28 January 1873. Sadly, it was demolished in 1978.

This postcard dates from 1904 and shows what St Leonard's church looked like inside. The sum of £7,000 was spent on purchasing the land and erecting the church.

Originally there had been a chapel on Millgate but in 1836 it was decided that there was a need for a larger place of worship. Consequently, Holy Trinity Catholic church was erected on Parliament Street.

The ornate interior of Holy Trinity Catholic church, which opened in 1836 after a building programme costing £3,000.

The building of the cemetery began on 23 February 1856 and, including the purchase of the land, cost £50,000. In 1877 the cemetery was extended to cover more than thirteen acres. This Edwardian postcard, addressed to Staunton Hall, shows the grounds after the second extension had been carried out in 1901.

THE METHODIST GUILD

Newark Sectional Rally

THURSDAY, FEB. 9TH, 1939
AT
BARNBYGATE CHURCH

VISIT OF THE

Rev. David R. Mace, M.A., B.Sc.
(Archway Hall, London)

Service 4 p.m.   Public Tea 5-15

Great Evening Rally
at 7 p.m.

Chairman—Mr. G. B. JARRATT (Nottingham)

ADDRESS by Rev. DAVID R. MACE

Don't miss this opportunity
for Fellowship and Praise

COLLECTION FOR EXPENSES

E. Stephenson, Printer, Barnby Gate, Newark

An advertisement for a Methodist rally which took place in 1939, shortly before the Second World War began.

William Becher Tidd Prath held the position of choirmaster at St Augustine's church between 1906 and 1956. A roll of honour for the choir hangs on the wall. To qualify for inclusion three years continuous attendance was needed. If six years unbroken service was achieved the reward was a solid silver watch and chain.

St Augustine's was originally a mission room of the parish church. It opened in 1886 and the final service was held in May 1998.

Christ Church, Newark

Lombard Street was the site chosen for Christchurch, which was built in the Early English style in 1836 at a cost of £3,000. The famous Newark MP, W.E. Gladstone, gave the church its first organ. Restored in 1880-81, the church became redundant in 1958 when a new Christchurch was opened in Boundary Road.

Situated on Barnby Gate, the New Methodist Connexion Chapel suffered extensive damage to its windows during a hailstorm on the afternoon of 11 July 1903. With stones up to an inch across reported, it is not surprising that so many windows were smashed.

Groups of people stand proudly with their banners representing Hawtonville Methodist School and Farndon Wesleyan Sunday School. The annual Sunday School Treat traditionally took place in the third week of June.

Children in their Sunday best on this postcard labelled 'nasturtums'. The judging of the floats took place in the Market Place before a procession set off around the town.

Floats drawn up in the Market Place with the business premises of J.T. Wilkinson and Curry's in the background.

A group of children wait patiently outside the Town Hall on float number nine, which was labelled 'Gems For his Crown'. This postcard was produced by J. and M. Simpson of Wilson Street.

A float in the 1914 Sunday School Treat drawn up at the corner of the Market Place with Bainbridge's in the background.

Porter's shop forms the backdrop in this view of the Market Place. Some proud salvationists pose for the camera.

Local photographer Frank Robinson took this picture as the floats in the Sunday School Treat made their way around the town. Some were horse-drawn while others, as here, were pulled by willing volunteers.

The pullers dressed in their best clothes must have found it hard work dragging the floats to their final destination, the Sconce Hills. This is another postcard produced by Frank Robinson.

Five
At Work and Play

The Old Grammar School situated on Appleton Street. Newark Grammar School was endowed in the reign of Henry VIII by the Revd Thomas Magnus, a local boy made good. The frontage seen here dates from 1817. The school moved to Earp Avenue in 1909.

The Magnus Grammar School, situated in the centre of town on Appleton Street, was convenient for access but only had limited accommodation and so, at the turn of the century, it was decided to relocate to larger premises.

The new Magnus Grammar School, seen here from the playing fields, was built on Earp Avenue and pupils transferred from the old buildings in 1909.

Magnus Grammar School's gymnasium. For many years the school enjoyed a wide reputation for the quality of its sports teams. One former pupil who went on to make a name for himself was the actor Sir Donald Wolfit.

Inside the assembly hall of the Magnus Grammar School, soon after it was opened. Initially, the new buildings catered for 30 boarders and 120 day boys.

In July 1883 the Free Library was presented to the people of Newark by William Gilstrap who belonged to the family of maltsters involved with Gilstrap, Earp and Co. He spent over £10,000 on its construction.

In 1931 a new Technical College and School of Art was built at a cost of £25,000. The site chosen was part of what had formerly been the Chauntry House grounds.

The Market Place has always been a natural meeting place for local groups. Here, Southwell photographer H. Barrett has recorded a gathering of Lord Harrington's hounds outside the Town Hall. Note the packed balcony.

An Edwardian gathering in the Market Place with everyone turned out in their Sunday best.

Newark FC from the 1904-5 season. This picture by Southwell photographer H. Barrett illustrates the length of shorts worn by football players in the early years of the twentieth century.

Newark FC from the 1907-8 season. The local football club, whose ground was off Muskham Road, had been formed in 1868.

Prior to the 1930s, when the citizens of Newark wished to swim outdoors they had to make use of a cordoned off section of the River Trent by Tolney Lane. It was then decided to provide a more salubrious venue.

In the era before television most entertainment had to be produced locally. A number of bands and musical groups flourished in Newark and the surrounding area including the Cameronian Carnival Band.

A group of buses stand ready for service outside the Castle Brewery on Albert Street.

Before the widespread ownership of cars many goods such as bread, fish, meat, milk and hardware were delivered door-to-door. Here, the local coalman James Widdison of 16 Friary Road has paused with his horse and cart outside the Gilstrap library in Castle Gate.

Many of the local population were engaged in brewing. This is a group of workers from Gilstrap, Earp and Co. posing with the tools of their trade: brushes, turning forks, turning shovels and tin shovels. The females wore split skirts so that their clothing did not impede their work.

James Hole and Co. was one of a number of local brewing companies. They began their imposing Castle Brewery on Albert Street in 1885 and used a variety of types of delivery vehicles over the years before they became part of the Courage group at the end of the 1960s.

Many companies have thrived in Newark by catering for the needs of the local farming community. T. Richmond and Son had a shop at 4 Boar Lane. The message on this postcard sent to Sibthorpe in 1912 reads, 'Regret we could not send the Goffering irons yesterday but will have them ready for you tomorrow'.

Beacon Hill rises to 148 feet above sea level. It was around this area of Newark that extensive gypsum quarrying took place.

Six

Around the Market Place

Newark Market Place and Town Hall

The Town Hall was constructed in 1772-73 by John Carr of York using local Mansfield stone for the facing. The most impressive room was the ballroom with its ornate ceiling.

The Market Place, *c.* 1904. The local artist H. Hadfield Cubley produced a set of six paintings of Newark which were reproduced as postcards by Raphael Tuck and Sons. This is his interpretation of the Market Place with the Moot Hall in the background.

Below the Town Hall was a covered market area to which entry was gained through the central arches.

The properties seen here to the left of the Town Hall were demolished in 1903.

Compare this view of the bank building to the left of the Town Hall with the previous photograph. This one dates from 1939.

At the side of the Town Hall is the half-timbered Queen's Head public house. This photograph can be dated to pre-1947 as the last door to the right of the Town Hall still provides access to the Borough Police Station, which transferred at this time.

A closer view of the Queen's Head when Florence M. Smith was the licensee. Next door the white fronted building is W.H. Ash and Son the bakers, flanked on the other side by J.T. Wilkinson the furnishers.

As well as a prestigious retail establishment in the Market Place, J.T. Wilkinson also had this warehouse and shop with access from round the corner on Church Street. This advertising postcard dates from before World War One.

Entry to Ash's yard was obtained by going through a narrow arch between the Queen's Head and Ash's bakers shop in the corner of the Market Place.

This postcard was published by M.E. Summers of Newark in the early 1930s and shows how the buildings in Ash's yard changed in appearance early this century. Today, with Ash's shop demolished, the Tudor building stands proud in the centre of the opened-up yard.

Parked close to The Queen's Head is a Pepper's delivery vehicle advertising 'organised daily services'.

Hearty Good Wishes for Xmas. and the New Year.

Newark Market Place and Church.

The Moot Hall, seen here underneath the church tower and next to the *Herald* newspaper offices, was built in 1708. The majority of town business was conducted here until the Town Hall was built in 1773. The Moot Hall was demolished in 1965-66.

CHURCH & MARKET PLACE, NEWARK, 882-10.

The *Newark Herald* newspaper, seen here operating from the Market Place shop of J. Stennett the printer and stationer, was founded in 1791 and published until 1960.

Market Place, Newark

On the opposite corner of Church Street to Stennett's was Curry's cycle shop. Cycling was one

No. 2422.

of the crazes in the Victorian and Edwardian eras.

The Moot Hall was part of the ground floor occupied by shops. To the left are the premises of A.W. Coyne. His radio and record shop has the famous advertising slogan 'his master's voice'. The dog and horn gramophone are prominent.

Porter's grocery business has been a feature of Newark for over a century. This shop on the corner of Bridge Street was purchased by George Howard Porter in 1893-94. George and his family built up an enviable reputation for the quality of their produce which is maintained today, even though the family connection was broken in 1968.

Ye Olde White Hart inn is said to have been built in 1413. It had a long history as a public house before eventually becoming a draper's and more recently a building society office. The little shop next to it is Stanley Noble's Pie Corner which was in business from the 1930s to the 1960s.

In 1867 John Cottam Bainbridge purchased Ye Olde White Hart and moved his drapery business into the premises, expanding upstairs and into adjacent buildings. He employed a number of people in both the retailing and manufacturing departments. The name continued long after the family sold up in the early 1900s.

71

The White Hart Yard. Behind the impressive frontage facing the Market Place was the more mundane range of buildings seen here.

The Saracen's Head was constructed in 1721 replacing an earlier inn. It served as a coaching inn for many years. Later, Bainbridge's expanded into part of it.

Like its neighbour, the Saracen's Head, the Clinton Arms building dates from the eighteenth century and replaces an earlier inn on the site. It covered a large area as there was a rear entrance for vehicles on Lombard Street. Previous names of this inn include The Cardinal's Hat, The Talbot and The Kingston Arms.

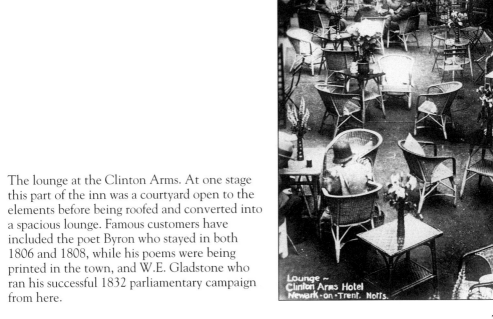

The lounge at the Clinton Arms. At one stage this part of the inn was a courtyard open to the elements before being roofed and converted into a spacious lounge. Famous customers have included the poet Byron who stayed in both 1806 and 1808, while his poems were being printed in the town, and W.E. Gladstone who ran his successful 1832 parliamentary campaign from here.

73

The photographer has captured an impressive group of motor vehicles parked outside the Clinton Arms Hotel. With so little activity on Stodman Street and in the Market Place, it might well be a Sunday or a public holiday.

In Edwardian times Newark continued to be a thriving market town with people travelling from outlying villages to sell their spare produce and other wares, and to buy provisions to take back with them.

Mayor's Sunday was an annual event in the life of the town. Here we see the official party leaving the Town Hall on 12 November 1905. This picture was taken by Howard Barrett of Southwell.

The Mayor of Newark greets Lord Harrington outside the Town Hall on 19 January 1906. In the background are some of the huntsmen about to accompany His Lordship as he sets out from the Market Place with his hounds.

Mr and Mrs A.M. Manderville ride through the streets of Newark. Manderville, who was a London financier, stood in the 1906 parliamentary election for the Newark seat, but lost by 328 seats to the local candidate Mr J.R. Starkey.

Mr J.R. Starkey on the steps of Newark Town Hall, giving his thanks to the voters of Newark for returning him as their MP in the 1906 election. He secured 4,772 votes against his rival's 4,444.

Seven
Central Newark Streets

The Palace Theatre and Appleton Gate. The advertisement at the Palace Theatre is for *The Student Prince*. The theatre was built by Mrs Emily Blagg in the early 1920s on land released after the demolition of the Chauntry House.

A variety of carts along Appleton Gate. Church Walk can be seen going off to the left by the lamp-post. There is a sign to the right advertising the Fox and Crown, a pub dating from 1794.

Appleton Street, c. 1950. This picture looks the opposite way to the previous one and dates from around forty years later. The transport has changed and note how the corner of Church Walk is now a tobacconists rather than a private house.

The pedestrian thoroughfare of Church Walk runs from Appleton Street down to the parish church of St Mary Magdalene.

A pen and ink drawing of Church Walk that was published by Whiles in 1905 and titled 'Newark Church from the Vicarage'. It is interesting to compare this artist's impression with the previous photograph.

The spire of the parish church stands guard over the cobbled Balderton Gate pictured here on a postcard produced around 1908 by local photographer, Davage.

Bailey's 'Cheap, General and Fancy Drapery Shop'. This is an advertising postcard produced to publicize the business that William Hefford Bailey ran at 2 Barnby Gate from around 1890 until 1910.

Bridge Street, Newark

Looking from the Market Place along Bridge Street, the first shop is Ridge and Co. the booksellers. The shop beyond is the Central Grocery Stores followed by J.A. Page, clothiers; the Cash Clothing shop; the Maypole Dairy; and John Mills and Sons Ltd, boot and shoe manufacturers.

81

An Edwardian view of Cartergate with the neighbouring public houses The White Hind and The New White Hart on the left. The tall building in the distance belonged to James Hole and Sons, brewers who supplied the White Hart and many other local pubs with beer.

Almost the same view as the previous picture but separated in date by around forty years.

Kirkgate, looking down towards the parish church. The art store of A. Jacobson is prominent on the left and facing it is a row of cottages containing a mixture of dwellings and shops. These were all demolished towards the end of the 1930s.

A little further down Kirkgate is the Old Kings Arms with the licensee H. Attenborough. This illustration comes from a postcard sent from Newark to Hyderabad, India, in January 1904 for the princely sum of 1d.

KIRK GATE, NEWARK ON TRENT

Another public house in Kirkgate was the Boar's Head where locally produced Hole's Ales were sold. Built on the corner of Middlegate and Kirkgate in 1883, it finally closed in 1959.

On the opposite corner of Middlegate from the Boar's Head was this Tudor-style building occupied by Simpkin's. Thankfully, this building is still with us.

The Tudor-style shop from the previous picture is now on the right as the Valentine and Co. photographer has moved a little further along Kirkgate. The white shop to the left belongs to the long established decorating company W.S. Heading and Son.

Kirkgate, Newark-on-Trent.

Looking up Kirkgate with St Mary's behind the photographer and the post office on the left. On the right are Lees and Sons, tobacconists, and W.S. Heading, decorators. Beyond is Shaw and Bailey who ran a pawnbrokers from these premises for many years.

newark.

Taken slightly further back from the previous picture, this photograph gives a better view of the half-timbered building which belonged to Lady Leake in the Civil War. It was also the lodgings of Queen Henrietta Maria when she stayed in Newark between 16 June and 3 July 1643.

The post office was designed by local architects, Saunders and Saunders, and built by George Brown and Son. It was opened in February 1908, replacing the post office in Cartergate.

LARGE SELECTION
POST CARDS,
VIEWS,
GOSS CHINA.

F. HENRY DAVAGE.

HIGH CLASS
LEATHER GOODS,
HANDBAGS, PURSES.

Whist Prizes, Fancy Goods.

KIRKGATE PRINTING WORKS, NEWARK.

An advertising envelope for F. Henry Davage of the Kirkgate Printing Works. Davage produced many postcard views of the town which were usually sold in sets of six in envelopes like this one.

The Wesleyan chapel and school on Barnby Gate. Designed by James Simpson, the chapel cost £5,261 to build and was opened on 2 July 1846. The writer of this postcard sent in February 1905 says, 'This is where the organ recital was held'.

Drawing back from the Wesleyan chapel this picture shows its unusual position, surrounded by establishments whose income was based on alcohol. The Rutland Arms is just a little further down the street, The White Horse is beyond that and facing the chapel was the Devon Brewery.

This view of Stodman Street from the Market Place presents a traffic-free scene. The Governor's House is to the left and the side of the bank to the right.

The Governor's House, Stodman Street. During the Civil War the Governor of Newark Castle, Sir Richard Willis, lived in this Tudor building. In Edwardian times Joseph Gelsthorpe ran the clothiers to the left while J.E. Thompson occupied the tobacconists to the right.

A post-Second World War view of the Governor's House in which Ernest E. Rick has taken over the clothiers and Lees and Sons are operating Ye Olde Governor's Tobacco Shoppe.

This view of Stodman Street from the Market Place by Newark photographer, Frank Robinson, has captured it decorated to celebrate the Coronation of 1911. The shop to the left belonged to Whiles the printers and stationers where the Byron Library could be found. A little further down is the Royal Oak.

The rear of the Governor's House. It was in this building that Prince Rupert famously quarrelled with Charles I in October 1645.

Stodman Street looking towards the Market Place. A postcard sent from Newark in 1916 with the Royal Oak, which was demolished in 1962, on the right and Boots the chemist on the left.

Lombard Street with the Beaumond Cross in the distance. Coming towards the camera is a motorcycle combination driven by a lady. Beyond the cross is the garage of Harrison and Co.

An unusual advertising card for Harrison and Co. the motor garage owners who were based at 41 Carter Gate. It is interesting to wonder how much this car would be worth today.

The Golden Fleece on Lombard Street was opened in 1790 and continued until 1933. The local Warwick Ales were sold here. The crowd is watching the first prize winner in the Sunday School Treat competition as it proceeds around the town.

The Notts. and Derbys. Band march down Lombard Street in 1930. In the background is the Golden Fleece public house where G.H. Cottam was the licensee at this time.

Lombard Street, *c.* 1920. To the left, beyond the Beaumond Cross, is the Robin Hood public house, which was built in the early eighteenth century, but with extensions that came later. To the right is the shop belonging to J.C. Kew, coal and coke merchants.

Robin Hood Inn on Lombard Street. This prominently situated inn began life catering for passing coaches by supplying accommodation for travellers.

Beaumond Cross after the railings had been removed. Its position at the junction of Cartergate, Lombard Street and Albert Street meant that it increasingly restricted the passage of traffic, resulting in its eventual removal to the gardens on London Road.

BEAUMONT CROSS, NEWARK-ON-TRENT

The Beaumond Cross from Lombard Street. A. Wadsworth's haberdashery and furniture shop is situated behind the cross.

This postcard was published by Hunt and Co. Central Studios, Newark. These impressively bedecked premises are thought to be in Newark, but still await positive identification.

Eight
South-East Newark

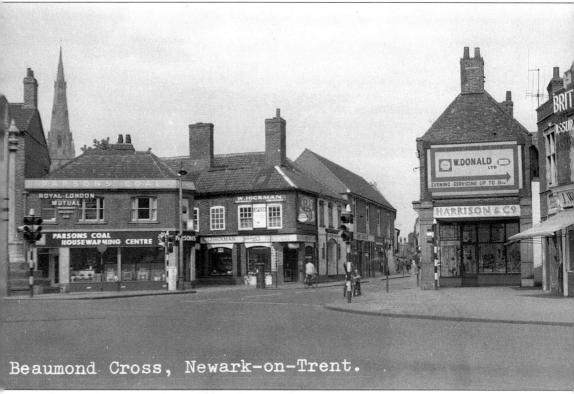

Beaumond Cross, Newark-on-Trent.

London Road commenced at Beaumond Cross where Lombard Street, Cartergate and Albert Street also meet. For many years the ancient cross was strategically placed at this intersection before being moved to its present site on London Road in 1974.

A pleasant site for the Municipal Offices situated at the far end of this park in London Road. To the left is the spire of St Mary's church. This photograph dates from the end of the 1940s. Since this date the new library has opened on the site.

London Road gardens from a different direction. The tall building in the distance is the Newark Hospital.

The Friary Gardens. The friary in Newark was home to a band of St Augustine monks but it fell victim to Henry VIII in the dissolution of the monasteries in the 1530s.

A traffic-free Friary Road. To the left the gates gave entry to a walled deer park that contained the early eighteenth-century Chauntry House which has now sadly been demolished.

The School of Science and Art was designed as a memorial for Queen Victoria's Diamond Jubilee and was opened by the Mayor, Dr F.H. Appleby on 28 October 1900. The art department occupied the top floor while the science department was based on the ground floor. From 1910 the Lilley and Stone School was based here.

During the Second World War many Polish nationalists, including pilots, fought bravely for the Allied side in the Battle of Britain. A number lost their lives including General Wladyslaw Sikorski, Chief Commander of the Polish Armed Forces Abroad, who died in a plane crash in August 1943. A number were buried here in Newark.

The open-air swimming baths. At the start of the 1930s these new open-air baths were opened at a site on Sherwood Avenue. They used an up-to-date design and provided both a safe and hygienic venue.

The swimming pool had a series of changing rooms built in the neoclassical style. At the deep end (8ft 6in) there was a large slide and a selection of diving boards.

A dispensary was founded in part of the Town Hall in 1813. This outgrew two sets of premises before the purpose-built hospital seen here was opened on 29 April 1881.

Newark Hospital at the beginning of the 1930s. It still retains its ornate railings which separated the grounds from the increasingly busy roads. These railings were sacrificed to the national need during the Second World War.

London Road at its junction with Baldertongate. The fountain central to this picture was provided by public subscription in memory of local woman, Ethel Harrison, who drowned on 7 December 1906 while saving a young boy from the Shropshire Union Canal. Designed by Saunders and Saunders of Newark, the fountain was unveiled by the Mayoress, Mrs O. Quibell, in August 1908.

A lone car travels down London Road towards its junction with Charles Street.

A quiet scene in London Road, close to Harcourt Street. There were a number of larger houses built in this area of the town.

No. 63, one of the large houses in London Road, in a picture dating from 1909. At this time it was not unusual for people to have postcards of their own residences produced for use in communicating with friends or trades people.

Nine

Around Newark
Part One

Main Street, Balderton

At one time, when travelling out of Newark on the London Road it was possible to see fields before reaching the village of Balderton. However, the increasing need for housing has meant that Balderton has significantly increased in size over the years. In 1801 its population was only 636. This had risen to 1,404 by 1891 and more than doubled again to 3,132 by 1921.

Main Street, Balderton. The schoolboy appears to be more concerned with the antics of the photographer than the contents of the shop window which seem to have captured the attention of the pair of ladies. Another woman crosses Main Street to join in the fun.

This view of Grove Street lacks much movement except in the far distance. In 1941 an airfield was opened in Balderton which partly explains the presence of Frank Whittle (later Sir Frank) in the village during the Second World War.

The building to the left is the Old Hall in Balderton. It was here that Sir Frank Whittle based himself in 1943 while working on designs for his prototype jet engine.

Balderton New Hall was constructed in 1840 for the local banker, Thomas Spragging Godfrey (1801-59), and was situated in a park extending to 135 acres. By the 1900s it had become the home of Newark brewer, William Deeping Warwick. In the 1930s it became a hospital.

107

Standing on the River Trent, Farndon has been an important crossing point of the river for many years. A ferry operated across the river close to the Britannia Inn which can be seen on the far bank.

Like many Trentside villages, Farndon was prone to flooding. Here, the bus that travelled between the village and Newark tackles the flood water in 1932.

This postcard, produced by M.E. Summers of Newark, was sent from the village post office in Farndon during September 1932. Note the post box on the wall of the thatched cottage adjoining the post office.

The Rose and Crown was one of two public houses that sold beers and spirits in Farndon in the 1930s. Situated next to the post office in the previous picture, it sold Hole's Newark Ales.

Flintham Hall and estate came into the hands of the Thoroton family in 1789. They in turn married into the Hildyard family and the Thoroton-Hildyards own Flintham to this day. In the 1850s the eminent Nottingham architect T.C. Hine was employed to update the hall.

T.C. Hine added Italianate fronts to the east, south and west sides of the hall. He also built the tower, seen here to the left, and the great conservatory on the right.

The stores in Flintham were run by Frederick Arthur White from August 1911 until he retired in March 1949. After this date his daughter took over until 1982. His legacy includes an extensive photograph collection showing the area and events that occurred there.

The schools at Flintham were built in 1873 at a cost of £1,000. The process of replacing them began in 1962 when the first phase of a modern school was opened in the village.

The original Stoke village was close to the church but in 1664 the plague struck, killing 159 inhabitants. As a precaution the village, which mainly consisted of wooden buildings, was burnt to the ground and the survivors rebuilt their homes on a new site closer to the Fosse Way, renaming their village East Stoke.

The final event in the War of the Roses took place on Stoke Field, close to East Stoke, in 1487. Troops loyal to King Henry VII met and defeated an army led by the Earl of Lincoln who was championing the claims of Lambert Simnel to the throne of England.

This early nineteenth-century bridge spans School Lane in East Stoke. It is quite a big structure to be found in a small village.

The vicarage at East Stoke. For many years this building housed the incumbents of the small church of St Oswald. An unusual grave close to the church tower belongs to Lord Julian Pauncefort who was the first British Ambassador to the USA. He died in Washington in 1902 and his body was brought back to East Stoke for burial.

Elston Towers was originally called Middleton Towers when it was built between 1872 and 1875 for Robert Middleton. Costing around £30,000, it consisted of a mixture of architectural styles and included an area designed as a Baptist chapel.

The tower was connected to the stable block of Elston Towers. It contained a clock with four dials which was driven by steam and able to play a variety of tunes on a series of bells. Sadly, the tower has now been demolished.

This postcard of Elston post office has a postmark on the reverse indicating that it was sent from the postbox in Elston on 20 July 1924 with its ultimate destination as Sneinton Dale in Nottingham. The cost of the stamp was 1d.

A group of local villagers have assembled in Elston for the photographer. Jasmine Cottage is to the left while the three people standing beyond the gate are in the garden of Dove Cottage.

Syerston Hall was a simple five-bay brick block building dating from 1795. This photograph was taken by Frederick A. White of The Stores at nearby Flintham.

In his King's England Series book on Nottinghamshire, Arthur Mee gives this picturesque description of the village of Syerston: 'Close to the Fosse Way but untroubled by its stir are its few farms and cottages with a tiny old church.'

Ten

Around Newark
Part Two

Like a number of Trent-side villages, Sutton on Trent has been prone to flooding over the years. Noteworthy floods this century include 12 August 1912 (seen here), May 1932 and March 1947. To help protect the village a flood bank was built in 1952 and a more effective one was erected in 1983.

M.R. Summers has travelled out from Newark to capture this watery scene on camera during the May 1932 floods. Here, some local residents have obligingly posed in the water outside The Lord Nelson Inn on Main Street. At this time the landlord was J.A. Parker. The writer of the postcard states, 'This is the way to our house from the Post Office'.

Sutton on Trent, The Mill & Mill House.

Sutton on Trent Windmill was constructed in 1825 and came into the hands of the Bingham family in the 1860s, remaining with them until they sold it in 1984. Originally it was a four-storey, black-tarred tower with four sails and an unusual six-bladed fantail. Like other windmills, it eventually succumbed to technology; sails were removed and a paraffin-driven engine fitted.

All Saints church in Sutton on Trent has parts dating from centuries ago. Up to the 1830s the tower was topped by a spire. The clock was fitted in 1911.

The school at Sutton on Trent was built in 1878 at a cost of £2,000. It had room for 170 pupils, a large proportion of whom have assembled in the road outside the school for this picture taken by Furniss of Sheffield.

Main Street, Carlton on Trent. Standing so close to the Great North Road, it is not surprising that Carlton on Trent became a stopping off point for people using the road. For many years the eighteenth-century Bell Inn, a large three-storey building with extensive stabling, catered for travellers.

The blacksmith's forge at Carlton on Trent is typical of a smithy with the large horseshoe design, decked out in dark brick to advertise its services to passers by. A similar structure can be seen at Gonalston.

Carlton on Trent Hall was built in 1765 by the Newark-based banker Joseph Pocklington.

A peaceful scene in Carlton on Trent, just prior to the First World War. Around this time the population numbered only 150.

The village of Cromwell lies to the side of the Great North Road, though this peaceful scene gives no hint of the bustle nearby. Amongst the trees the church of St Giles can be seen. This has parts dating from the fourteenth and fifteenth century, but owes much to the restoration that took place from 1873 to 1876.

This postcard of Cromwell was sent from Newark to North Muskham in December 1905. The lady cyclists, seen in the previous picture, have obligingly dismounted for the photographer. The man with the brush is again present. J.T. Spittlehouse of Alfreton took the photograph.

Caunton Manor dates from the early eighteenth century but was extended in the early twentieth century and 're-Georgianised' by Houfton whose changes included new windows to the side seen here and a large stone porch.

The most famous former resident of Caunton was Samuel Reynolds Hole. Born in 1819 he spent his childhood at Caunton Manor and later returned, first as curate, and then as vicar of the village church. He was fascinated by roses and became the first president of the National Rose Society. He was given the nickname 'The Rose King' by the poet Tennyson. In 1887 he became Dean of Rochester and died in 1904.

The Royal Oak Hotel on the High Street in Collingham is beyond the horse and cart. The hotel dates from the seventeenth century when wide roads were not so important. It has had to survive more recent suggestions to demolish it to improve traffic flow through the village.

Collingham Cross was erected in the fourteenth century. In this view from Edwardian times, it stands proudly outside Davies' cycle shop, which later became a garage catering for the new invention, the motorcar. In 1970 the cross was moved to a different site on the opposite side of the road.

The Crown Inn stood a little further down the road from the stone cross in the previous picture. In 1904, when this picture was taken, the landlord was William Smith and he sold Davy's Newark Ales.

This view of Bog Cottages, Collingham, is more typical of Venice than rural Nottinghamshire. Like nearby Sutton on Trent, Collingham was prone to flooding. This photograph was taken during the floods that occurred in May 1932.

Newcastle Arms and Ferry House, North Muskham. Until the 1940s a ferry operated from here to the village of Holme. The Newcastle Arms was built in 1692, but today it is known as the Muskham Ferry.

Most villages had small shops like W. Bennett, the grocer, which sold a wide variety of provisions. In the window are adverts for Royal Daylight lamp oil and the *Newark Herald* newspaper.

The small village of Kelham stands by the River Trent, which can be crossed in the village via a narrow stone road bridge. Close by is this ornate entrance to the grounds of Kelham Hall. For many years Kelham Hall was owned by the Sutton family who later became the Manners-Suttons.

Kelham Hall was designed in the Gothic style by the architect George Gilbert Scott. It replaced an earlier hall which was badly damaged by fire in November 1857.

In 1903 the Society of the Sacred Mission took over Kelham Hall and turned it into the headquarters of their Theological College.

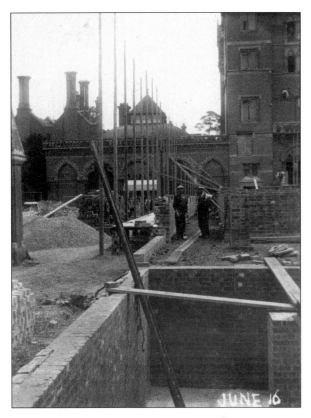

When the Society of the Sacred Mission acquired Kelham they embarked on a programme of extensions including residential accommodation and a chapel which was topped with a huge Byzantine dome. This was completed in 1928.